CANADA

TIGER BOOKS INTERNATIONAL

Text
Beth and Peter Duthie

Design
Patrizia Balocco

Map
Arabella Lazzarin

Contents

A land of majesty.................................*page 28*
Cities that reach to the sky...................*page 64*
The call of the land............................*page 84*
Life at the top of the world...................*page 102*

2-3 *The gentle brush of autumn tints the Laurentian Highlands near St. Adolphe d'Howard in Quebec's Parc des Laurentides. The worn down, comfortable terrain of the Laurentians is part of the oldest landscape in Canada. It is also the wilderness that Canadians from the highly populated areas of Quebec and Ontario enjoy every season of the year.*

4-5 *A skiff of snow covers one of the most photographed sights in Canada - the view of Lake Louise from the palatial Château Lake Louise. Named to honour Queen Victoria's daughter Princess Louise, Lake Louise is one of the gems of Banff National Park, Alberta, Canada's first national park.*

6-7 *Most of Canada was once covered by glaciers such as this one in Kluane National Park, located in the southwest corner of the Yukon Territory. Where debris flows forward from the two glaciers, it joins together to create a distinctive land form known as* medial moraine.

8 *Perched high in a spruce tree, a bald eagle (Haliacetus leucocephalus) surveys his domain. An ever-watchful hunter, this majestic bird of prey symbolizes the freedom of the wilderness.*

9 *The spectacular South Nahanni River, which runs through Nahanni National Park in the Northwest Territories, is one of the few remaining untouched rivers in North America. Accessible only by air and by non-motorized water transport, Nahanni National Park has been declared a United Nations World Heritage Site.*

12-13 *The rose-tinted light of early morning is reflected off the buildings of Toronto, Ontario, Canada's largest city and its financial capital. At 1800 feet, the CN Tower on the left is the tallest free-standing structure in the world.*

14-15 *Under the brilliant blue of an Alberta sky, boxcars await their load of grain near Champion. Now disappearing monuments of the Canadian prairies, the grain elevators next to the railway line inspired early twentieth-century architectural figures such as Gropius and Le Corbusier.*

16-17 *The extraordinary achievements of bush pilots flying small planes like this one changed the way of life in Canada's North and were instrumental in overcoming the challenges of travel in the country's more remote areas. The highly skilled pilots fly in the most severe weather conditions in small planes that land on water or on snow.*

This edition published in 1994 by
TIGER BOOKS INTERNATIONAL
PLC , 26a York Street Twickenham
TW1 3LJ, England.

First published by Edizioni White Star.
Title of the original edition:
Canada, ai confini del grande Nord.
© World copyright 1994 by Edizioni
White Star, Via Candido Sassone 22/24,
13100 Vercelli, Italy.

ISBN 1-85501-479-3

Printed in Singapore by Tien Wah Press
Color separations by Magenta, Lit. Con.,
Singapore.

ARTIC OCEAN

BEAUFORT SEA

BANKS ISLAND

ALASKA

VICTORI

YUKON

Mackenzie River

GREAT BEAR
LAKE

NOR
TER

▲
KLUANE NATIONAL PARK

GULF OF ALASKA

● WHITEHORSE
● CARCROSS

ST. ELIAS MOUNTAIN

MACKENZIE MOUNTAINS

MACKENZIE

● YELLOWKNIFE

GREAT SLAVE
LAKE

ALEXANDER
ARCHIPELAGO

BRITISH
COLUMBIA

▲ WOOD BUFFALO NAT

CARIBOU
MOUNTAINS

ATHABASC
LAKE

CREE
LAKE

PACIFIC OCEAN

COAST MOUNTAINS

ROCKY

ALBERTA

● JASPER

VANCOUVER
ISLAND

YOHO NATIONAL
PARK

● EDMONTON

SASKATCHEW

BANFF NATIONAL PARK
▲

● VANCOUVER

▲
SELKIRK
MOUNTAINS

● BANFF

● SASKATO

● VICTORIA

● CALGARY

MOUNTAINS

● CHAMPION

● REG

UNITED S
OF AMERI

Introduction

Consider a country and invariably the first thoughts that come to mind are of its people and their customs. A simple remark about France could evoke a Gallic shrug. The thought of Britain might conjure up an image of the proverbial "stiff upper lip." At the mention of India or the countries of the Far East, one thinks immediately of their enormous populations. But when most people think of Canada, their thoughts turn first to the land, the vast, almost indefinable geography. One of the largest countries in the world, Canada covers a staggering 3,8 million square miles. This landscape is what is initially so impressive about Canada. Indeed everything that is Canada is a product of this land. The very essence of being Canadian is to be found in the land.

Imagine taking careful steps along a poorly defined trail in a forest dense with tall stands of timber and lush with a ground cover of wet ferns and moss. The sound of a twig snapping underfoot resonates through the trees, filling the air with a deep, hollow sound that startles a Great Grey Owl. Barely moving his enormous wings, he takes flight over your head. This is a Canadian experience.

Imagine breathing the salty air of the open Pacific as you stand, feet chilled, at the water's edge, watching the breakers crash thunderously upon a seemingly endless sandy beach.

Imagine kneeling in a canoe at dawn, your paddle motionless as you watch a family of moose feed a short distance away from you along the edge of the lake.

Imagine the horizon on the prairies, dividing in elemental simplicity the burnished gold of wheat ripe for harvest and the unmarred blue of the sky. The sweet scent of clover fills the air and only the hum of crickets breaks the silence.

Imagine the chill of a winter afternoon in the mountains. Your face almost burns from the cold and your legs are weary from carrying you more than 15 miles on touring skis. A deer, seeking refuge for the night, darts across the trail into the forest.

It is moments like these - or the knowledge that moments like these do exist - that connect Canadians to their land.

Canadians understand that, economically, their future depends on weakening this connection. The land has traditionally been a major source of the country's wealth. The people have formed families of loggers, miners, fishermen, ranchers, oil men, and farmers. They know that they must establish a more diverse economy, one that is not as tied to primary industries. At the same time, they are aware that the rich farm lands, mineral deposits, oilfields, and fishing grounds will continue to play a significant role in their country's economic well-being, as will the growing tourist industry. Canadians know that they can never turn their backs on a land that is so generous.

The Canadian landscape also plays a major role in shaping the consciousness and psyche of its people. Even though the vast majority of Canadians live in an urban setting - and 30 per cent of the entire population makes its home in just three cities: Toronto, Montreal and Vancouver - many are still aware that a raw, untamed wilderness exists just fifteen minutes to three hours from their doorstep. There is a knowlege in most Canadians that beyond the city lies both profound beauty and a brooding danger that demands their respect.

With the wilderness so close at hand and a climate that can be so extreme, life for Canadians is rarely predictable. What is served up to them on a silver platter one day can be taken away the next. Consider the extraordinary gift of a hot summer's day. Huge white clouds hang in a brilliant blue sky. The breeze blows softly through meadows of wild flowers, and the air is alive with bird song. The day is long; dusk does not fall until 10 pm. The children glow from a full and wonderful day of outdoor play, and parents must struggle to get them into bed. All of this is cherished because of the realization that winter is to come. Canadians, then, can be seen as a stoic people. Conservative by nature, cautious of unnecessary risks, somewhat resentful of their lot, yet quick to display a quiet, stubborn pride in their country.

Canadians can grumble with the best and complain about the cold. They all have those moments when they feel as the early English settler, George Calvert, did before he moved south to Virginia. He found Canada - or at least the eastern part he was familiar with - to be a

"wofull country" with the "sadd face of wynter" upon it for more than half the year. This feeling is still held by many who leave Canada for warmer climates, or who migrate to the southern United States as soon as the trees are bare of leaves and return only when they come to bloom again in spring.

When the winter is at its most severe, it can and does drive the population indoors. In Newfoundland, for instance, where George Calvert attempted settlement, the residents may find the snow packing up to their roof lines. And no right-thinking rural driver would set out on the shortest winter journey without emergency supplies. Cold weather draws people together. There is an air of survival to this togetherness, a true generosity of spirit that emerges the further the thermometer dips into the minus degrees celsius. Still, there are few who can remain unmoved by the first snow, when the land is transformed before their eyes, the trees become crystalline sculptures, and the falling snowflakes scatter the sunlight like fairy dust. Winter then becomes a time of magic.

While the cold robs Canadians of any possibilities of glamour they might have, forcing them into bulky down-filled coats, mitts, and knitted caps or "toques" to prevent frost-bitten ears, for many, winter is a time of exhilarating outdoor activity. From the Arctic Circle to Northern Ontario winter lovers take to their motorized sleighs called "Ski-doos" (a Canadian invention) and explore frozen lakes and deserted mountain roads. Many head for the hills to ski in some of the most spectacular mountain scenery in the world, or to ride down the banks of a frozen river. Other lace up their skates. Whether it be on a pristine mountain lake high in the Canadian Rockies, along a frozen canal through Canada's national capital, Ottawa, or on one of thousands of small outdoor rinks across the country, skaters find renewal in the joy of fluid motion. Young boys emulating their heroes in the National Hockey League wield their hockey sticks around community rinks and dream of the day when they, too, will hoist the Stanley Cup high overhead on victory night.

The harshness of the climate and the rugged immensity of the landscape have also always dictated the pattern for settlement in Canada. Though most Canadians would be the first to tell you that they come from the world's largest country, a country that is thirty-three times the size of Italy, their reality is, in fact, quite the opposite. When Canadians reflect on their country, they usually think of it in terms of their own region; the country is simply too large to grasp as a whole. The irony of their situation lies in the very roots of the word Canada. The early French explorer Jacques Cartier gave the name Canada to his settlement on the St. Lawrence River, having derived the word from a native term meaning "village." Of course, the name was later applied to the whole of British North America, which included the areas that now make up seven of Canada's ten provinces as well as the Northwest Territories and even the entire northern half of North America beyond the 49th Parallel, still today the world's largest undefended border.

This "village" is a long, thin strip that hugs the border. Thus, a more accurate way of describing the country's true size - and the area of its greatest population - is through the image of a clothes line that stretches from the Atlantic Ocean in the east to the Pacific Ocean in the west. Along this line are placed a series of clothes pegs, each of them representing one of Canada's major cities. At first the pegs appear relatively frequently, starting in the east with St. John's, Newfoundland, then moving along to Fredericton, New Brunswick; Charlottetown, Prince Edward Island; Halifax, Nova Scotia; Quebec City and Montreal, Ottawa and Toronto. The distance between the pegs begins to increase as the line stretches west to Winnipeg, Manitoba, spans the prairies to Regina, Saskatchewan, and Calgary, Alberta, until finally after one more thousand-mile stretch the last peg is reached: Vancouver and Victoria, British Columbia. The vast majority of Canada's population of almost 27.5 million lives along this clothes line, within a few hundred miles of the Canada-United States border.

This metaphoric clothes line actually approximates the route of the Canadian Pacific Railway, which began as a miraculous promise from the Canadian government to encourage the territory of British Columbia to enter the confederation. The railway was one of numerous efforts to unite this enormous, disparate land and bring together its people. Unfortunately, the construction of the Trans-Canada Highway, a subsequent attempt to bridge those same gaps, hastened the decline of rail travel in Canada. Completed in 1962, the Trans-Canada Highway spans 4,850 miles and takes in the breathtaking range of landscape between St. John's,

18-19 *A thriving fishing and trading post in the 1700s, the settlement of Mingan, Quebec, is situated in one of North America's wildest areas, the Mingan Archipelago. It is still reachable only by air and by sea.*
Even in mid-summer, the last traces of an iceberg drift down from the North Atlantic.

20-21 *Angel Glacier is situated on Mount Edith Cavell, Banff National Park. Nowhere is the force and the grandeur of nature more apparent than in Canada's mountainous areas. For the thousands of visitors who come from around the world to explore the Canadian Rockies, the experience is unforgettable.*

22 top *Hunting and trapping played a key role in the development of Canada and continue to be a way of life, primarily for the natives in the North. Animal pelts are at their finest in the winter months, when the hunter must make his way through the wilderness by snowshoe. This traditional hunter's cabin is in the Yukon Territory.*

22 bottom *Of all the men who sought their fortune in the 1896 Klondike Gold Rush only a handful were laid to rest under tombstones such as this one in the cemetery in Carcross, Yukon Territory. The vast majority of them returned home, having made just enough to cover their expenses with a little to spare.*

23 top *Gold mines like this one, the Giant Gold Mine near Yellowknife, Northwest Territories, once flourished in Canada's North. It was the discovery of gold that led to the settlement of British Columbia and the Northwest Territories, and rich mineral deposits continue to be a primary source of wealth in the North. Turn-of-the-century fortune-seekers came for gold; in the late twentieth century, diamonds are the lure.*

23 bottom *Steam wheelers were critical in bringing supplies up the rivers of Canada's North. This one now lies aground at Carcross, Yukon Territory.*

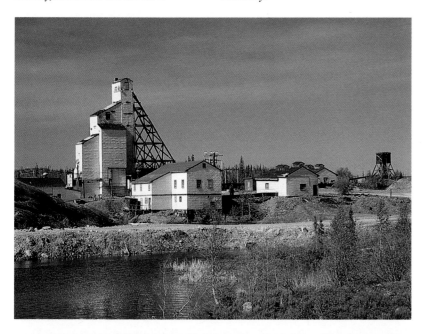

Newfoundland, and Victoria, British Columbia. While the railway and the highway sought to tie the country together geographically, the Canadian Broadcasting Corporation was formed to unite the country culturally. Established with government funding in 1936, the C.B.C. is now one of the most widely respected public broadcasting systems in the world, and along with the scarlet-coated Royal Canadian Mounted Police and the buffalo, one of Canada's most potent international symbols.

Yet where most see unity, there has always been and always will be diversity. This cultural richness goes back as far as 9,500 B.C. - when the first of Canada's indigenous people made their way across the bridge of land that connected Siberia to North America and developed a network of productive, complex cultures - and continues now because of the interplay of cultural influences from around the world. As a result of its immigration policies over the last century Canada has become home to Ukrainians, Czechs and Slovaks, Poles and Hungarians, Serbs and Croats, who were instrumental in settling the Canadian prairies; to Asians, especially the Chinese who came to Canada to work in the gold fields and on the construction of the Canadian Pacific Railway; to Italians, who now represent one in every five inhabitants of Toronto; to Americans, who came to seek their fortune in the rich farm and cattle grazing land of Alberta; to Sikhs from India, who came as British subjects seeking a new life, first in the West Coast timber industry, then in their own businesses; and to people of countless other nationalities.

To the outsider, Canada may appear to be politically and socially stable and, in fact, a bit dull. Unlike the United States, Canadians have no revolutions to spice up their history classes. They did successfully repel American forces in the War of 1812, but that was fifty-five years before the British North American Act offered them nation status in 1867 and they were officially Canadians. The "shoot 'em up wild west" history depicted in the movies was less of a reality in Canada than it was in the country's more boisterous neighbour to the south. But the struggles that Canada is destined to face are more likely cultural and social ones. Beneath its bland exterior, Canadian society is turbulent and dynamic. It lives under the constant threat of division as the independently-minded province of Quebec strives to find its comfortable fit within

Canada's social fabric. So far, in the face of confrontation, the Canadian urge is to talk, to negotiate, to find within the British parliamentary system of debate and diplomacy a middle road, and so discussions with Quebec and negotiations with Canada's native peoples continue, not without anger or frustration, but in a context of peace.

In much the same way, Canadians continue their dialogue with the land. Recognizing that it is fruitless to defy nature, they seek instead to make peace with the land - and in doing so they are able to reap its abundant rewards. Join a conversation between Canadians and what are they likely to be talking about? The sun could be shining, a nearby window could open onto a variety of spectacular views, and yet the discussion could easily focus on bad weather. Indeed, Canadians do have some cause to complain about the severity of the winters and the unpredictability of the weather in general. With an average year-round temperature of minus 5.6 Canada, ranks as the coldest country in the world. However, meteorologists tell us that, by their definition, most places across Canada usually experience only a handful of truly awful days per month in any given winter. Canadians can take some solace in the knowledge that it does get colder in Greenland and Siberia. Still, it is little comfort to the people of Ottawa to know that the only capital city in the world colder than their city is Ulaanbaatar, Mongolia.

While the earth receives an average of only five per cent of its precipitation as snow, more than one-third of Canada's annual precipitation comes in this form. Montreal, for instance, has the dubious honour of receiving more snow than any other city of its size in the world. Montreal's municipal government budgets $50 million per year for snow removal, and each year snow ploughs remove more than 40 million tonnes of snow from the city's streets. Ironically, along with other North American children, the children of Montreal probably have visions of Santa Claus a (Père Noël) snowbound at the North Pole, yet the High Arctic is a particularly dry area. At the weather station in Alert, Northwest Territories, just 447 miles from the North Pole, the average annual snowfall is only about 59 inches, and the rainfall amounts to less than 20 mm.

The winds really can howl. On remote Ellesmere Island what is known as a "cow storm" is a gale force wind strong enough, as the locals

24 *A rekindling of interest in native culture is drawing many young people back to the traditions that tie them to their past. This young Plains native proudly wears a costume worn at gatherings such as this one held in Saskatoon, Saskatchewan, and recaptures the colours of the traditional dyes and the original quillwork designs.*

say, to "blow the horns off" the muskoxen. In Newfoundland they have their equivalent - a "wreckhouse" - a fierce wind that has been known to blow trains off tracks and, presumably, to wreck a few houses along its way. Just as the French have their *mistral* and the Alps has the *foehn*, Canada has the warm *chinook*, a native word meaning "snow-eater." Some legends have likened the strong, dry westerly or southwesterly wind to "the warm breath of an Indian princess." When this princess breathes in mid-winter, Alberta's temperatures rise dramatically, melting snow, exposing the ground for grateful herds of cattle, and sending excited children outdoors in their shirtsleeves. The *chinook* is merely the best known of Canada's winds: scores of others exist, many of them with colourful names. In the north a warm, dry spring wind is known as a "break-up wind" because it speeds up the break-up of ice on rivers and lakes. A sudden wind that arises on a calm day is referred to as a "fairy wind."

If it is not the weather dominating their discussion, it could be issues of identity. While inhabitants of other countries may quarrel from a position of fierce national identity, affirming with every statement just who they are, the Canadians are constantly grappling with questions of self-definition - not who they are but who they are not. Historical examples of this struggle abound, and they remain for many years in the collective memory of Canadians. After Canada gained its independence from Britain in 1867, for example, the country's official flag continued to be the British Union Jack. In 1925 Canada's tenth prime minister, William Lyon Mackenzie King, created the first committee to investigate possible designs for a new flag, one that would stand as a symbol of Canada's nationhood. Although the matter was brought up in Parliament many times over the next few decades, it was never resolved. The issue gradually became a controversial and divisive one, reaching a head in the early 1960s. In December of 1964, after almost six months of heated debate in the House of Commons and at kitchen tables across the country, Canada had its own flag - a red maple leaf centred on a white field and set off by red bands at each end. Thirty years later there are still Canadians who maintain the flag should never have been changed.

By virtue of its location on the other side of the 49th Parallel, the United States has played a key role in Canada's identity crisis. Canadians may envy the bravado of American nationalism and the extensive domestic market that their neighbours to the south enjoy, but they are quick to leap to their own defence when labelled as Americans by others who fail to see major differences between the two nationalities. As a result, Canadians are the first to boast that accomplishments such as the variable pitch propeller, the electric cooking range, and the world's first steam-operated fog alarm are the product of Canadian ingenuity, obscure as some of those inventions may be. Canadians lay claim, too, to the invention of the telephone. Never mind that Alexander Graham Bell came to Ontario from Scotland with his family in 1870, when he was in his early twenties, and that much of his work on the telephone was done with a co-worker in Boston! Yet Canadians are justifiably proud to claim that it was their countrymen who gave the world the game of basketball and the indispensable zipper, and it was Canadians who developed the process to produce paper from wood pulp, created the first electron microscope, developed kerosene oil, and invented the halftone for reproducing photos in newspapers. Standard Time, the system of measuring time used all over the world, was developed by a Canadian surveyor and railway engineer. Thanks to another Canadian invention, the Canadarm, astronauts in the U.S. space shuttle are able to handle and repair satellites and objects in space. Healthy diabetics around the world owe their health and their increasing longevity to the Canadian physician who was the co-discoverer of insulin.

If you ever sit down with a group of Canadians, they are easily distracted from their complaints and insecurities. You will find they will wax eloquent about hockey - a Canadian invention, of course - and you will soon discover that far from lacking a sense of identity, Canadians exhibit a quiet pride, a product of their turbulent but committed relationship to their land.

A land of majesty

28 top *The landscape of the Yukon Territory is dotted with numerous rivers and lakes such as this one, the Kluane Lake in Kluane National Park. The Yukon is one of two territories in Canada's North, and it is the country's most western point. Those who make their home in the Yukon take advantage of what the area has to offer, spending much of their time in the spectacular outdoors.*

28 bottom *Once referred to as the "Gateway to the Gold Rush," the Yukon Territory takes its name from the Kutchin Indian name for the Yukon River.*
Called Yu-kun-ah, or "great river," it drains over two-thirds of the Territory as well as part of British Columbia and much of Alberta. Just as San Francisco made its mark during the California Gold Rush, the Yukon acquired its colourful reputation from the Klondike Gold Rush of 1897-99. When the world "discovered" the Yukon it was through the exploits of its rough and tumble adventurers and its equally daring officers of the Royal Canadian Mounted Police, the scarlet-coated lawmen who "always got their man."
In fact, the brash young land they heard about was one of the first parts of North America to be inhabited by humans.
The hunting ancestors of today's Yukon native people have been in the area since approximately 8000 B.C.

29 *Lake O'Hara is a pristine mountain lake nestled in the high altitudes of Yoho National Park, just across the Alberta border in British Columbia. It is a hiker's delight, with many well-maintained trails and awe-inspiring vistas.*
Discovered by explorers seeking a route to the Pacific, Yoho was named after the Cree word meaning "awe."

30-31 *Glistening sunlight illuminates the Victoria Glacier above Lake Louise in Banff National Park, Alberta. The ice wall in the centre of the photograph is over 329 feet thick.*

31 *On a grey day, a single ray of sunlight breaking through the clouds will bathe the Rocky Montains in enchanting light.*

32 *Featured on Canada's one cent coin, the Beaver (Castor canadensis) is a symbol of hard work, gnawing enormous numbers of trees to build dams and form ponds like this one.*
It was also the single most important element in Canada's development, since it was the hunt for Beaver that opened the West. The animal's fur was especially prized in Europe, where the beaver hat was a mainstay of many an elegant gentleman's wardrobe.*

33 *The Black Bear (Ursus americanus) is one of three types of bears found in Canada's forests and the one most often spotted by hikers. An unassuming, mainly solitary animal, the Black Bear will rarely attack. It is seen from coast to coast, unlike the Grizzly and Kodiak Bears, which are found only in the West.*

34-35 *The reclusive young Great Grey Owl (Strix nebulosa), a resident of the northern forest, is one of fifteen species of owl found in Canada, and with a wingspan of over 5 feet, the largest North American owl. Like other owls, the Great Grey Owl has acute hearing and is an impressive hunter. It feeds on small mammals,* particularly voles, and it will swoop down to snatch one of the creatures that it has heard moving under the snow. Its hearing is enhanced by its flattened, parabolic-shaped face, which serves to capture sounds. The Great Grey Owl is considered to be less aggressive and more approachable than the Great Horned Owl.*

The silence of nature

36 *During the summer months much of the Yukon Territory is green and lush. The landscape of the Yukon was carved by glaciers, and glaciers still cover many of the highest mountain peaks in the area. The broad, U-shaped valleys were caused by the gouging action of the glaciers as they moved down river valleys. The small lake in the left foreground, a kettle lake, would have been formed by the melting of an ice block.*

37 *Vegetation is scarce in the region of the southern Arctic, the northernmost area of the Yukon. Only low bushes, such as dwarf willow and birch, and ground cover such as lichens, grasses, mosses and sedge will grow here. The green in this photograph is sedge that "floats" on a permafrost base. The intriguing polygonal shapes were formed by the alternating freezing and thawing of the land's surface.*

38-39 *The Yukon is an unspoiled land isolated from the rest of Canada by rugged mountains. Wildlife abounds here and continues to be an important part of the natives' livelihood. Sealed from the moderating effects of the Pacific Ocean, temperatures have been known to drop to -63 degrees Celsius, yet they will climb to as high as 35 degrees celsius in summer. During what became the world's greatest gold rush, the population of the Yukon swelled to 40,000, but scarcely more than half that number live here today. Three out of every four residents live in the largest city, Whitehorse, about 62 miles north of the border to British Columbia.*
The rural areas remain virtually unpopulated, attracting tourists from around the world much as the Gold Rush did a century earlier.

40-41 *The St. Elias and Coast Mountain chains in the Yukon Territory include some of the highest mountains in Canada and extensive polar ice fields that cut off access to the Pacific Ocean. Viewed from above, the glacial debris on Kaskawulsh Glacier resembles a moving river of ice. The area where the fresh snow meets the melting glacier is known as the "fern line." Although tourism is one of the Yukon's main sources of revenue and*

the number of visitors to the area is growing steadily, only the most ardent climbers and expeditionists would venture into this region.

42-43 *Covering an area of over 10,810 square miles, Great Slave Lake, Northwest Territories, is one of the largest freshwater lakes in the world. For eight months of the year, it is covered in ice. The spring break-up heralds a season of high activity when the land comes alive. Nothing is more important to the people of this area: after months of darkness and isolation, they are able to connect - if only briefly - with the rest of Canada.*

Land of water and ice

44-45   *Wood Buffalo National Park, Canada's largest national park, straddles the border between Alberta and the Northwest Territories. Its arboreal forest is a haven for wildlife of all kinds, including 4,000 Wood Bison (Bison bison), called buffalo, and the rare Whooping Crane (Grus americana), fewer than 200 of which exist in the wild.*

45   *The wilderness in Canada takes countless forms, but there are few as austere as these deserted salt plains in Wood Buffalo National Park, Northwest Territories. Looking strangely like snow on a warm summer day, the salt makes for a stark and foreboding contrast between land and sky.*

Nature
in the wild

46 *It is not unusual to see Moose and other wildlife rambling along backroads or through the woods just a short distance from the highway traffic. The forest fires that sweep through Canada's dense forests are a rejuvenating force that increases grazing territory for ungulates such as the Moose.*

47 *Millions of Plains and Wood Bison (incorrectly called buffalo) once roamed the prairies, but when Wood Buffalo National Park was formed to protect the Wood Bison in 1922, the number of Wood Bison had been reduced to a few hundred. A herd of Plains Bison was also relocated to the area several years later, and today there are more than 4,000 bison in the park. The largest of Canada's mammals, the bison was the primary means of survival for the native peoples of the West. Knowing that the bison is easily frightened, the natives initially hunted the animals by driving them to the edge of cliffs, or buffalo jumps, from which they would plummet to their death. The natives depended on the bison for food, used the animal's sinew and bones to make tools and weapons, and made clothing and tipis from the skins. They wasted nothing. But it was after the opening of the West that the number of bison declined precipitously. After 1850 the animal hides were even used as drive belts in machinery.*

48-49 *Originally there were said to have been four arches carved by the sea in Le Rocher Percé, a 1675-foot long rock off the tip of Quebec's Gaspé Peninsula, but only this one impressive arch remains. One of the area's key tourist attractions, Le Rocher Percé is also an important bird sanctuary.*

50-51 *Some of the richest fishing grounds in the world are to be found in the waters off Newfoundland. The seafaring men who make their living there are dependent on lighthouse posts like this one on one of the many tiny, remote islands off the coast. Most of these lighthouses are now automated.*

Life close to the ocean

52 Found only along the Atlantic Coast, the Gannet breeds in dense colonies on steep cliffs or cliff tops on Quebec's Gaspé Peninsula and in Newfoundland and Nova Scotia. Reaching up to 40 inches in length, this large marine bird is pure white except for its gold cap and black markings around its pale grey eyes. It rarely strays from the sea. On hunting expeditions its streamlined body can reach speeds up to 60 miles an hour as it plunges 100 feet into the sea, diving deep into the waves for fish.

53 *Thousands of Gannets are to be found on the cliffs of Cape St. Mary's, Newfoundland, and on Quebec's Île Bonaventure, the largest gannet colony and a game sanctuary. Both male and female Gannets are identical in colour.*

The female lays a solitary egg each year in its seaweed nest, sharing the incubation with her partner for 43 days. Not unlike many retired Canadians, the Gannet winters on the Florida coast and in the Gulf of Mexico.

54-55 *Cradled by the rugged shoreline of the Avalon Peninsula on Newfoundland, the town of Conception Bay was founded before 1800. For most of its history it depended on small boat, inshore cod fishing and some farming. Now many of the townspeople commute to the nearby capital of St. John's to work, while the residents of St. John's make the trip to the beaches of Conception Bay in the summer months.*

56-57 *The barren winter landscape of the tundra near Churchill, Manitoba, bursts into colour in the summer. In September the Arctic ground cover turns a brilliant crimson. It is the land's last display of extravagance before the snow comes. The rocks in the foreground are Precambrian, the oldest land formation in the country.*

The colourful palette of Quebec

58-59 *Clouds settle over the St. Maurice River, which flows into the heart of Quebec, the Laurentian Highlands of La Maurice National Park. The rugged beauty of this area is a result of glacial activity that scraped and carved the many small, pure lakes and youthful rivers. Most of the highlands are covered with black and white spruce, balsam fir, tamarack, maple, poplar and white birch which turn to magnificent yellows, oranges and reds before the winter snows take hold of the land. With a climate too hostile for agriculture, this area has long been recognized as a wonderful recreation area. Vacationers from Ottawa, Montreal, Quebec City and cities in the United States flock here to stay at cottages or to camp, fish, hunt, swim or sail in summer and fall, and to skate, snowshoe or snowmobile in the winter. Not only do these forests yield the national emblem - the maple leaf - which is proudly displayed on the Canadian flag, they also provide the favourite treat of many Canadian breakfast tables: maple syrup.*

The link between
water and land

60 *A lighthouse search and rescue station offers safe passage to the many deep-sea fishing trawlers and oil tankers that travel up and down the treacherous shoreline of the west coast of Vancouver Island, British Columbia. Once seen as an idyllic existence, the way of life of the lighthouse keepers was the stuff of legends. They lived alone on remote islands that were often a great distance from shore, worked around the clock to stoke the lamps with fish or whale oil, and ensured the safety of passing vessels. Many of them rarely ventured to the mainland, and those who had families frequently educated their children themselves.*
With the advent of automation, all of this has changed. The lighthouse keeper has been replaced by equipment that is maintained by visiting technicians, and most of Canada's lighthouses are now unmanned.

61 top left *Long Beach is one of three sections of Pacific Rim National Park, established in 1970 as a marine reserve. The dense rain forest in the park is populated with Black Bear, deer, Cougar and martens, while the sea is home to Grey and Killer Whales, Harbour Porpoises, sea lions and Sea Otters. Until the early 1970s, the park was virtually inaccessible. Now it is a popular destination for hikers who come to tackle one of the most challenging hiking trails in North America, the West Coast Trail, which evolved from the old search and rescue trail that clung to the coast.*

61 top right *The Killer Whale (Orcinus orca) returns each year to Johnson Strait off the coast of British Columbia. The whale became a symbol and totem for the North West native people.*

61 bottom *Queen Charlotte Island National Park is separated from the northern coast of British Columbia by 30 to 80 miles of open sea. The Queen Charlottes are among the most isolated islands in Canada and home of the Haida peoples.*

62-63 *The legendary Niagara Falls, on the border between Ontario and the United States, has been a favourite tourist destination for longer than Canada has been a country. The word Niagara stands for "thunder of water" - and the most thunderous waters are on the Canadian side. In the upper left of the photograph is the "Maid of the Mist," the popular cruise boat which provides a thrilling but damp experience for many of the more than 12 million visitors who come to the Falls each year. The first "Maid of the Mist" was launched in 1846, in the days before they had outlawed the stunts for which the Falls became notorious. Thrillseekers set off over the Falls in boats and barrels, or walked over them on tightropes. One daredevil Frenchman even crossed the gorge by tightrope carrying a man on his back.*

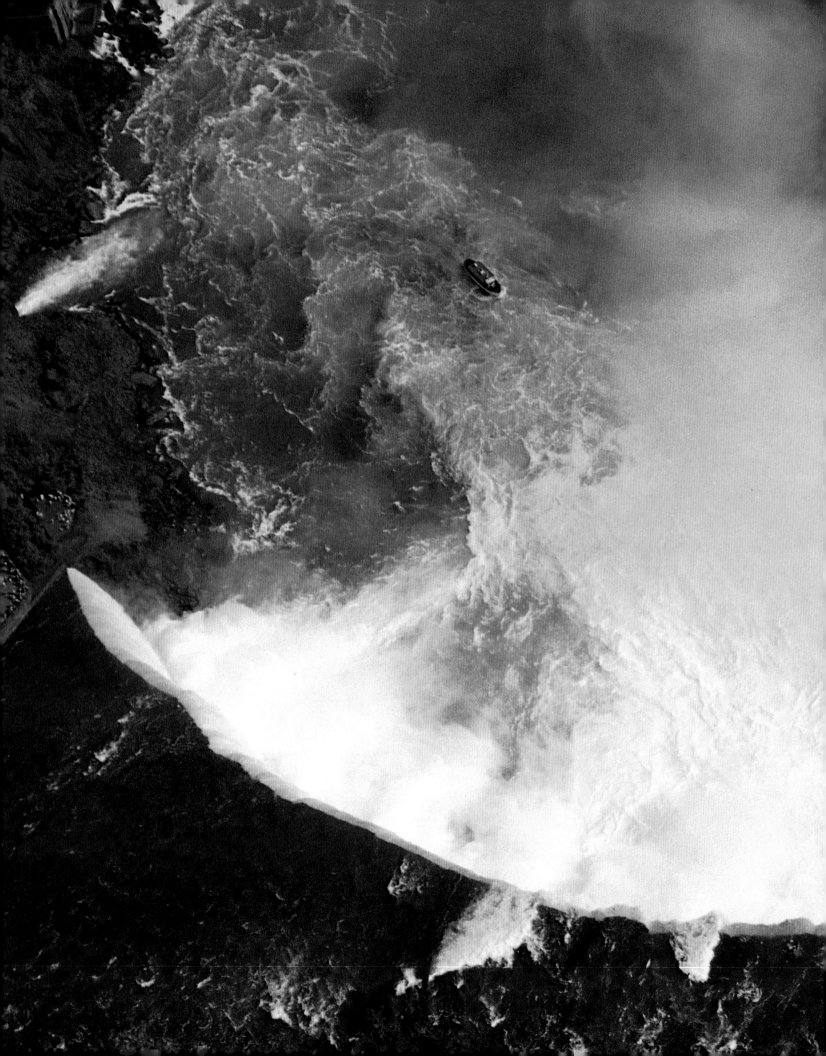

Cities that reach to the sky

64 top *The price of a bus fare buys a ride on the "sea bus" that links downtown Vancouver with North Vancouver, across the Burrard Inlet. The twin-hulled catamaran is an integral part of Vancouver's public transit system.*

64 bottom *The illustration shows part of the Parliament Buildings complex in Ottawa, Ontario, with the Centennial flame in the foreground. The Parliament Buildings have been the seat of Canada's federal government since Canada became a nation in 1867. This building, the Parliamentary Library, was the only one to survive the fire that razed the original Parliament Buildings in 1916. A splendid example of the Gothic revival archictectural style, it was modelled, as were the original buildings, on the Houses of Parliament in London and was intended to illustrate the constancy of British traditions from the medieval period to the present.*

65 *This picture presents the Legislature Building in Victoria, British Columbia. Victoria was incorporated as a city in 1862, during the reign of Queen Victoria. A popular tourist and retirement spot, the city is situated on a peninsula at the southern tip of Vancouver Island and is blessed with a mild climate. In February, while other Canadian cities are blanketed in snow, Victoria holds its annual blossom count.*

Toronto: modernity and tradition

66 *A city of contrasts, Toronto is an exciting blend of modern and traditional architecture. The glass and steel towers of Canada's most important financial institutions dwarf this Victorian flat-iron building, a reminder of the city's more humble beginnings. As well as being a key international financial centre, Toronto is also a large employer of the manufacturing industry. One in every three Ontario workers is employed in the city's factories.*

67 top *Ontario's Legislature Building, built in Toronto in 1892, is one of a number of interesting heritage buildings in the city.*

67 bottom *One of the most distinctive municipal buildings in Canada, Toronto's City Hall was designed by Finnish architect Viljo Revell in 1965. The two curved towers and the domed, circular council chambers in between stand out in a skyline otherwise dominated by more conventional buildings. The plaza opposite the buildings has become a favourite skating rink in winter.*

68-69 *Stretching along the shores of Lake Ontario, Toronto, Ontario's capital city, glows in the sunset. Prominent landmarks are the Skydome, home of one of the city's greatest sources of pride, the Toronto Blue Jays, and the CN Tower on the left.*

Vancouver,
the Canadian jewel

70 top *In recent years Vancouver has emerged as an important member of the Pacific Rim Community, but the city's large "Chinatown" has long been one of Vancouver's most colourful and vibrant attractions. Day and night, it is a focal point for the city's rapidly growing Asian population.*

70 bottom *The Vancouver skyline seen from Stanley Park. Vancouver's equivalent of New York's Central Park is an oasis of green just minutes from downtown. Stanley Park's forest, jogging and cycling paths, zoo and aquarium make it a favourite with visitors and residents, many of whom start their day with a walk or run around the park's sea wall. The city's picturesque setting often prompts comparison with another Pacific Rim neighbour - Sydney, Australia.*

71 *In the picture one can see Vancouver's City Hall. Incorporated in 1886, Vancouver is Canada's third largest city and arguably the most desirable place to live in the country. High land values have now obliged much of the city's population to live in the growing suburban municipalities of the Lower Mainland.*

72-73 *Vancouver at its finest, with Stanley Park and the north shore mountains in the background. Located in the hub of the city's harbour, Canada Place Hotel and Convention Centre, built for the World's Fair held in Vancouver in 1986, is also the departure point for luxury liners that sail the Pacific waters. The raw piles of sulphur on the barges that can be glimpsed in the distance are another fact of day-to-day life in this busy harbour city - and a reminder of Canada's primary resource-based economy.*

74-75 *The downtown of Vancouver, British Columbia, fluorishes after a rare snowfall. It is a point of pride to Vancouverites that they can spend the morning skiing in the nearby mountains, then head to the beach for a stroll in the sun.*

Quebec, the city of ice

76 The Citadel at Quebec City was once referred to as "The Gibraltar of North America." It was built between 1820 and 1831, when Quebec City was Canada's main port. Although it was designed to protect the city from enemy forces that might come up from the St. Lawrence River or from the Plains of Abraham (in the foreground), it was never attacked. It continued to be the headquarters of the commander-in-chief and the centre for the defence of all of British North America until the last of the British troops left in 1871. Canada's Governor-General at the time, Lord Dufferin, persuaded city officials not to dismantle the walls, and the Citadel is now a museum and tourist attraction.

77 The major centre of French culture in North America and the oldest city on the continent, Quebec City retains an enchanting old-world charm.
Bundled up against the cold, visitors come to the ciy each year in February to explore its streets and join in the festivities of the annual Winter Carnival - the street music and parties, feasts, children's hockey tournament, parade, races, and ball. One of the most popular of these events is an international snow sculpture competition, held since 1973. A key attraction is the snow castle of the Carnival's giant snowman mascot, Bonhomme.

Montreal, the city on the hill

78-79 *As the sun sets on Montreal, the most vibrant French centre in North America comes to life. A sophisticated, cosmopolitan city, Montreal is a lively blend of the French and English cultures and an exciting commercial centre with a decidedly French flair. It is renowned for its cultural offerings, its active night life, and its varied international cuisine.*

Cities of enchantment

80-81 *Often called the "Gateway to the West," Winnipeg, Manitoba, is proud of its rich ethnic diversity.*

81 top *One of North America's oldest cities, St. John's, the capital city of Newfoundland, has been an important sea port since the early 1500s.*

81 bottom *The Legislature Building in Edmonton, Alberta, overlooks the city's picturesque North Saskatchewan River valley.*

82 In summer, small boats cruise the 125 miles of the Rideau Canal, which connects the Ottawa River with Lake Ontario.
In winter, the stretch of the canal that ends at Ottawa's Parliament Buildings freezes to become the world's longest skating rink. Built between 1826 and 1832 as a means of transporting troops to the St. Lawrence River if Canada were to enter into another war with the United States, the canal has been used only for peaceful purposes.

83 *On a clear day the snowcapped Rocky Mountains beckon the visitor to Calgary, Alberta.*
The Calgary Tower on the left looks out over the mountains to the west, while the view to the east is of the province's vast prairies.

Until the discovery of major oil fields in Alberta in the late 1940s, Calgary was a ranching and meat-packing centre. Now it is referred to as the "Houston" of Canada, a major energy centre that houses the head offices of countless oil and gas companies.

The call of the land

84 top *Once the main means of transport for the native populations and a key element in opening up Canada to settlement through fur trading, the canoe has become a popular part of Canadians' recreational time. Here a group of canoeing enthusiasts set off along the "route de la Métabeskéga" in Quebec. These ribbons of waterways formed the trading network for the native peoples and the* coureurs des bois *(runners of the woods), who learned the native tongues and the ways of the wild.*

84 bottom *While the* coureurs des bois *"ran the rapids" in primitive canoes, these white water rafters use inflatable rafts to take canoeing to the limit, navigating a series of rapids on the Ottawa River.*

85 *A park warden patrols the hills overlooking Indian Snake River in one of the most remote areas of Jasper National Park, Alberta. Canada has more national park areas than any other country in the world. The wilderness park of Jasper is famous for its soaring mountains, dense forests, and glacier-fed rivers and lakes. The pack-horse is still the only effective means of travelling in back country like this in western Canada's national parks.*

The endless prairies

86 *The farm was an instrument of early settlement in Canada. During the 1870s, immigrants from around the world hungered for peace and the rich farmlands that symbolized freedom to them. The first collective settlements began in 1874. Mennonites - a religious group dating back to the Anabaptists of the early 16th-century Reformation in Europe - left the Russian steppes because of religious persecution and began what was later seen as a unique contribution to Canadian farming. Their experience in Russia had taught them to dry-land farm without the need of a nearby river, something that earlier settlers had thought to be necessary. Today colonies of Mennonites from numerous countries farm successfully and preserve their customs. Some, such as the Swedish Mennonites, still practise traditional farming methods.*

87 top *In Saskatchewan the prairies stretch endlessly. It is a region of sky and an ever-moving "sea" of wheat. Since the development of cold-resistant strains of wheat, the Canadian prairies have become one of the major grain producers in the world.*

87 bottom *Today the family farm in Alberta still symbolizes a traditional life of hard work and wholesome family values. It can be a harsh life, but it is not without its rewards. It is a world away from the din of urban development; a life beneath a sky of ever-changing drama.*

The Graneville fishing area

88 Despite the modern technology of depth sounders and radar equipment, the success of a West Coast fisherman still depends on his ability to read the water. Increasing fishing restrictions have constricted the fishermen's range and the period of time they are allowed to fish.

89 West Coast gillnetters and trawlers line the harbour near the Granville Street Bridge in Vancouver, a sheltered deep-sea port that gives fishermen easy access to the Pacific Ocean. Some of these fishermen find a popular outlet for their catch at the busy Granville Island Market located next to the harbour.

King salmon fishing

90 *East Coast fishermen haul in their catch as greedy seagulls await the scraps. For hundreds of years, fishing has been the way of life for many Maritimers. Now massive depletion of the fishing stocks is threatening their livelihood.*

91 left *Young children of the Yukon Territory admire their father's catch of king salmon from the Teslin River.*

91 right *Newfoundland cod fishermen carry on the now threatened tradition that has survived for centuries on the Grand Banks off Newfoundland's coast. This cod will go to market fresh, frozen, salted or smoked.*

The land besieged by cold

92-93 *In winter, when a storm rages, rural areas can seem even more remote.*

93 top *On extremely cold days, the combined effect of temperature and wind, the "wind chill," can freeze exposed skin in minutes.*

93 bottom *During the long winters on Hudson's Bay in Churchill, Manitoba, the pick-up truck and ski-doo become important means of transportation.*

The bold rodeo cowboys of Calgary

94 *They still call it "The Greatest Outdoor Show on Earth" - and it's all because of the cowboys. At Alberta's Calgary Stampede, held each year in July, cowboys become entertainers to the world, showing their skill in an exciting array of events that includes saddle bronc riding, steer wrestling, and calf roping. The horses used in the saddle bronc riding event (left and below) are bred specifically to test the cowboys' prowess.*

95 A saddle bronc rider must remain in the saddle until the buzzer sounds after what seems like a lifetime but is really only eight seconds. In a tribute to traditional ranching practices, modern-day cowboys also demonstrate skills that were once all in a day's work: roping calves and wrestling steers. The stakes may be high, but so are the rewards. Cowboys now travel from all over North America to participate in what has come to be known as one of the most prestigious and lucrative rodeo competitions on the continent.

Games on ice

96 top *Living in a land ruled by winter - a land "where winter is king" - one soon learns to enjoy it. For many Canadians winter becomes a time to take part in what might seem like rather extreme outdoor sports and recreational activities. In Quebec City a team competes in an iced river canoe crossing, an annual event across the St. Lawrence River.*

96 bottom *A ski-doo, called the motorbike of snow machines, speeds across the winter landscape.*

97 top *Many young Canadians like this boy spend countless hours at hockey arenas, dreaming of a career in the National Hockey League, or skating with friends at an outdoor community rink, imagining the day when they will hoist the Stanley Cup overhead.*

97 bottom *A motor enthusiast takes to the ice on a specially equipped motorcycle in an event held in an indoor arena in Vancouver, British Columbia.*

98-99 *High above the clouds, a solitary telemark skier makes his way through the Selkirk Mountains of British Columbia.*
The hoarfrost on the trees creates ghostly hoodoos in an area that boasts some of the most spectacular helicopter skiing in the world.

100-101 *Emulating the great cowboys of the West, outdoorsmen on horseback enjoy a mild winter day as they gallop through freshly fallen snow in the Quebec forest.*

Life at the top of the world

102 *The Arctic Fox (Alopex lagopus) is found throughout Canada's far North, living in the arctic tundra all year round. Its fur turns snowy white in winter, protecting it from predators. Smaller than the other fox species, the Arctic Fox feeds on small mammals and on carcasses left by wolves and Polar Bears.*

102 bottom *Insulated by a thick layer of fat beneath their wrinkled skin, a group of Walrus (Odobenus rosmarus) reclines on an ice floe in the Northwest Territories. The Inuit used the Walrus in much the same way that the Plains Indians used the bison - wasting nothing. The Walrus was hunted for its meat and for its oil, which was used as fuel. From the Walrus skin the Inuit made coverings that protected their boats from being destroyed by jagged ice.*

103 *Fearless and omnivorous, the immense Polar Bear (Ursus maritimus) is the absolute monarch of the North. It roams the ice and hunts seals in the winter months, waiting to catch them when they surface for air. The bear's thick fur and layer of fat (blubber) enable it to be comfortable for long periods in the frigid water. Man may be the main threat to the Polar Bear, but he is also, occasionally, the animal's victim.*

104-105 *In most areas, world-wide protests have brought the sealing industry to a halt. In eastern Canada the industry was based primarily on Harp Seals (Phoca groenlandica) such as this seal pup in the Gulf of the St. Lawrence River.*

The wild nature of the cold land

106 *Cape Graham Moore, Bylot Island, is in the Northwest Territories A British sea captain, Robert Bylot, sailed with explorers Henry Hudson and William Baffin in the early part of the seventeenth century. The island that was named after him is largely uninhabitable, with its steep mountainous regions, glaciers, and a coast that is difficult to navigate. Today Bylot Island is primarily a bird sanctuary.*

107 top *Wolves (Canis lupus) once roamed over many parts of North America. They have now been eliminated from settled areas and are found mainly in the wild areas of Canada's North. They feed mainly on small rodents, but a pack of Wolves could also bring down the weakest Moose in an area.*

107 bottom *For roughly 100,000 years the plant-eating Muskox (Ovibos moschatus) and its predecessors have made the arctic tundra their home. During the winter months, this relative of the mountain goat looks for food in areas that the wind has cleared of snow. Many of them starve to death before the winter is through.*

108-109 *What is most startling to urban visitors to the Northwest Territories is its silence and its vastness. Here the vista is disturbed only by the arrival of a fox.*

The Inuit of the Canadian Arctic

110 *For 2000 years Inuit hunters have depended on the Eskimo sled dog to transport them and their kill across the barren snowfields of the Canadian North. Each dog is capable of pulling between 100 and 180 pounds of weight on hunting trips that could require distances of up to 60 miles. Despite a harsh climate and the unavailability of food, the Eskimo sled dog possesses a loving nature. The dogs are important companions on hunts, providing company and support to the hunters by locating seal holes and holding Muskoxen and Polar Bears at bay while the hunters move in for the kill. Once thought doomed to extinction by the invention of the ski-doo, the dogs have proved themselves to be more reliable and more cost-effective than machines.*

111 top *June in the Arctic still provides enough snow for this sled and team to cross the iced sea near Melville Peninsula. A primitive breed, the Eskimo sled dog is carnivorous, feeding on the meat of Caribou, seal, fish and Walrus. The dogs have, however, an extraordinary ability to continue day after day with little or no food. A hunter's life depends on his dogs, and he will treat them like children or valued servants. The Inuit often named their dogs to honour dead relatives.*

111 middle and bottom *Stopping at night in the "Land of the Midnight Sun," the tired dogs feed and rest after a long day of hard work. In the 1920s the number of sled dogs in the North had reached in excess of 200,000, but by 1970 their population had dwindled to 200 pure-bred dogs. To prevent the dogs from becoming extinct, a new breeding colony was created from a few remote camps in Baffin Island and the Melville Peninsula. Twenty years later the colony still thrives.*

112-113 *On his journeys in the Arctic in search of a sea passage through the Arctic Archipelago, Sir William Edward Parry (1790-1855) became the first European to use the Eskimo sled dogs as a means of travel in the North and noted their exceptional qualities.*

114 *A young Inuit child plays outside in his fur coat.*

115 left *Inside a tent over an iced sea, an Inuit father feeds his baby under the watchful eye of an older sibling.*

115 right *An Eskimo woman tends to her child and prepares a tool made with a Caribou bone.*

116-117 *Dressed as always for the cold, two young friends share the playground at the top of the world.*

Igloolik,
the extreme
North

118 *On a June day, two Inuit women walk into the town of Igloolik on the Melville Peninsula, carrying their babies on their backs.*
The Inuit have been living in this area since about 2000 B.C., with the first "white man," or qallunaaq, having arrived in 1613.
Though their housing is more modern, today's residents of Igloolik survive as their ancestors did - by hunting, fishing and sealing.
This way of life is now severely challenged, as sealing and trapping become contentious issues around the world.

119 left   *A fishing boat awaits the summer thaw in the iced sea near Igloolik on the Melville Peninsula, Northwest Territories.*

119 top right   *A focal point in this remote settlement is the Hudson's Bay Company store, the oldest incorporated joint-stock merchandising company in the English-speaking world and an institution across Canada.*

119 middle right   *Seal skins are stretched and dried outside an Inuit house.*

119 bottom right   *A Polar Bear skin hangs from the porch railing of a more modern home in Igloolik. Resting against the porch is a stretched seal skin.*

120-121 *The settlement of Igloolik, Melville Peninsula, Northwest Territories, glitters in the soft twilight of an endless day.*

121 *This colourful warehouse at Nanisivik on Baffin Island, Northwest Territories, houses lead and zinc collected from some of the rich mines of the Arctic.*

Summer in the Canadian Arctic

122 Baffin Island is the largest island in Canada and the fifth largest in the world. The small settlement of Pond Inlet is directly across from Bylot Island, seen here behind a skiff of clouds. Situated at the northern tip of Baffin Island, Pond Inlet is named after Peter Pond, who saw the enormous economic potential of the North and became a well-known, active trapper.

Pond Inlet is, in fact, one of Canada's most northerly communities. Here sealing is still the primary source of revenue. During the endless sunlight of the summer months, children show no regard for conventional time schedules. They eat and sleep when they need to, and it is not uncommon to see children playing and visiting together outside at three o'clock in the morning.

123 top Located near the northeast head of Frobisher Bay at the southern tip of Baffin Island, the town of Nanisivik is an Inuit fishing village as well as a transportation and communications centre for the eastern Arctic. Searching for a northwest passage to the Pacific in 1576, Martin Frobisher was the first European to make contact with native populations here.

123 bottom *A young girl and her baby sister go out for a walk in Nanisivik.*

124-125 *The arrival of spring in Hudson Bay is cause for celebration, for the enormous inland sea (317,500 square miles) is covered in ice for most of the year. Native people have lived around the Bay for thousands of years, surviving by hunting and fishing. Here a young mother carries her baby in a traditional coat called a "parka." Small children ride along with their mothers inside the coat or in the hood.*

126-127 *Clouds and snow blanket Ellesmere Island, Canada's third largest island and its northernmost point. The island was named after the Earl of Ellesmere, who explored the region during the nineteenth century. Here small numbers of Muskoxen and Caribou eke out their survival along with small populations of Wolves, Arctic Fox, Weasel, Arctic Hare, Lemmings and some species of birds.*

Photo Credits:

Marcello Bertinetti / Archivio White Star:
Cover, pages 1, 6-7, 20-21, 22 bottom, 23, 28, 36, 38-39, 40, 41, 42-43, 44, 45, 47, 64 top, 70 top, 71, 74-75, 88, 89, 97 top, 110, 111, 112-113, 114, 115, 116-117, 118, 119, 120, 121, 122, 123.

Ken Balcomb / Bruce Coleman:
Page 61 top right.

Franco Barbagallo:
Pages 8, 9, 22 top, 33, 46, 52, 61 bottom, 62-63, 64 bottom, 72-73, 81 top, 84, 85, 86, 87, 90, 91 right, 92, 93, 94, 95, 100-101, 108-109, 128.

Erwin and Peggy Bauer / Bruce Coleman:
Pages 102 top, 106, 107 top.

Carlo Borlenghi / Sea & See Italia:
Pages 96 bottom, 97 bottom.

G. Boutui / Explorer:
Page 80-81.

Bill Brooks / ZEFA:
Page 78-79.

Fred Bruemmer / Bruce Coleman:
Pages 107 bottom, 126-127.

Bob & Clara Calhoun / Bruce Coleman:
Page 56-57.

Damm / ZEFA:
Pages 12-13, 65, 66, 68-69, 82.

Nicholas De Vore / Bruce Coleman:
Page 54-55.

Pierre Diot / CEDRI:
Pages 60, 61 top left.

Halle Flygare / Bruce Coleman:
Page 37.

Jeff Foott /Bruce Coleman:
Page 104-105.

Cesare Gerolimetto:
Pages 4-5, 30, 31, 70 bottom.

Cesare Gerolimetto / SIE:
Page 67 top.

François Gohier / Ardea London:
Page 103.

Marlin W. Grosnick / Ardea London:
Page 26-27.

Fr. Jourdan / Explorer:
Pages 2-3,48-49, 58-59, 76.

Kitchin / ZEFA:
Backcover, pages 14-15, 81 bottom, 83.

Gilbert Kiner / CEDRI:
Pages 18-19, 53.

Todd Karol / Agenzia Masi:
Page 24.

Mehta - Contact / Grazia Neri:
Page 16-17.

Patrick Morrow / Agenzia Masi:
Page 91 left.

Patrick Morrow / Overseas:
Page 98-99.

David Nunuk / Agenzia Masi:
Page 25.

Andrea Pistolesi:
Pages 77, 96 top.

Plisson / Explorer:
Page 50-51.

Fritz Pölking / Overseas:
Page 102 bottom.

Norbert Rosing / Overseas:
Pages 34-35, 124-125.

Gérard Sioen / CEDRI
Page 67 bottom.

G. Stott / ZEFA:
Page 29.

Johnathan T Wright / Bruce Coleman:
Page 32.